Contemporary

Abortion

John Stott

Marshalls
and
The London Institute for Contemporary
Christianity

Also by the same author in this series:

A Call to Christian Leadership
The Authentic Jesus

Marshalls Paperbacks
The London Institute for Contemporary Christianity
12 Weymouth Street, London W1N 3FB
Marshall Morgan and Scott
Marshall Pickering
3 Beggarwood Lane, Basingstoke, Hants. RG23 7LP, UK

Extracted from *Issues Facing Christians Today* by John Stott
First published in 1984 by Marshall Morgan and Scott Publications Ltd
Part of the Marshall Pickering Holdings Group
A subsidiary of the Zondervan Corporation
This extract first published 1985
Reprinted
Impression number
86 87: 6 5 4 3 2

ISBN 0 551 01195 5

Phototypeset by Input Typesetting Ltd, London
Printed in Great Britain by Stanley L. Hunt (Printers) Ltd,
Rushden, Northamptonshire.

Introduction

'Contemporary Christianity', which is the concern of the London Institute, the annual London Lectures and this series of booklets, is not a new brand of the Christian faith which we have invented. On the contrary, what we mean by it is historic, biblical Christianity creatively applied to the contemporary world with its complex questions of social, sexual, medical and personal ethics. The aim of these Contemporary Christianity booklets, therefore, is to help Christians to think about the issues of the day from a Christian perspective.

But has the Bible anything to say about our modern dilemmas? Yes and no. No, in the sense that it does not contain slick solutions to current controversial problems. Yes, in the sense that it contains God-given principles of thought and action. By absorbing these we can develop a Christian mind, with which to think about even the most 'secular' topics of today.

Is it our responsibility, though, to busy ourselves with social questions? Should we not rather concentrate on evangelism and leave social action aside? Certainly evangelism remains a top priority for all Christians; we are under orders to spread the good news of Jesus Christ throughout the world. Yet Jesus himself did more than preach the good news of God's kingdom; he demonstrated its arrival by good works of love and power. So words and works should go together in our Christian service too. And we cannot act socially if we do not first think socially. Our evangelical forebears in the eighteenth and nineteenth centuries have left us a wonderful example of their combined evangelistic and social concerns. For the first half of this century, however, we somehow managed to mislay our social conscience. Now that we are gradually recovering it, we have much catching up to do.

Here is another question in the minds of many Christians: since the west has become so secularized, can we hope to impose our Christian standards on a non-Christian society? No, 'imposition' is the wrong word. Nevertheless, we can commend them, and can deploy every possible argument in the process, believing as we do that God's law is not only good in itself but good for human beings and for human society. In a democracy changes in legislation depend on consensus. Our Christian duty therefore is to get into the debate and seek to influence public opinion towards approving and desiring God's way. Even fallen human beings perceive that justice is better than oppression, compassion than callousness, and cooperation than confrontation.

God give us in this generation more Christian leaders with a sensitive conscience, a clear mind and a courageous heart!

JOHN STOTT

The Abortion Dilemma

The debate over abortion is admittedly complex. It has medical, legal, theological, ethical, social and personal aspects. It is also a highly emotional subject, for it touches on the mysteries of human sexuality and reproduction, and often involves acutely painful dilemmas.

Yet Christians cannot opt out of personal decision making or public discussion regarding this topic merely because of its complexity. Instead, two factors should bring it to the top of our agenda.

First, what is involved in the abortion issue is nothing less than our Christian doctrines of both God and man, or, more precisely, the sovereignty of God and the sanctity of human life. All Christian people believe that Almighty God is the only giver, sustainer and taker-away of life. On the one hand 'he himself gives all men life and breath and everything else', and 'in him we live and move and have our being'. On the other, as the psalmist says to God, 'when you take away their breath, they die and return to the dust'. Indeed, whenever anybody dies, Christian faith struggles to affirm with Job: 'The LORD gave and the LORD has taken away; may the name of the LORD be praised.'[1] To the Christian, then, both life-giving and life-taking are divine prerogatives. And although we cannot interpret 'you shall not kill' as an absolute prohibition, since the same law which forbade killing also sanctioned it in some situations (e.g. capital punishment and holy war), yet the taking of human life is a divine prerogative which is permitted to human beings only by specific divine mandate.

Without this, to terminate human life is the height of arrogance. Hence Mother Teresa's strong feelings about the evil of abortion:

'. . . only God can decide life and death. . . . That is why abortion is such a terrible sin. You are not only killing life, but putting self before God; yet people decide who has to live and who has to die. They want to make themselves almighty God. They want to take the power of God in their hands. They want to say, "I can do without God. I can decide." That is the most devilish thing that a human hand can do. . . .'[2]

Next, the question of abortion concerns our doctrine of man as well as of God. For, however undeveloped the embryo may still be, everybody agrees that it is living and human. And in whatever way we decide to formulate the relationship between newborn and unborn children, our evaluation of human being is inevitably involved. Therefore the present practice of almost indiscriminate abortion reflects a rejection of the biblical view of human dignity. It is this aspect of the situation which most concerned Francis Schaeffer and Everett Koop in their book and film *Whatever Happened to the Human Race?*, which related to infanticide and euthanasia as well as abortion. They rightly traced 'the erosion of the sanctity of human life' to 'the loss of the Christian consensus'.[3]

So then, if both divine sovereignty and human dignity are being challenged by the abortion debate, no conscientious Christian can stand aside from it.

The Revolution in Public Attitudes

The second reason for taking the issue seriously concerns the revolution which has recently taken place in public attitudes. Whether or not doctors have actually subscribed to the ancient Hippocratic Oath (fifth century BC), it has been generally assumed that they took its main undertakings for granted:

'I will follow that method of treatment which, according to

my ability and judgment, I consider for the benefit of my patients, and abstain from whatever is deleterious and mischievous. I will give no deadly drug to anyone if asked, nor suggest any such counsel; and in like manner I will not give to a woman a pessary to procure abortion'.

Since some other clauses of the Oath are decidedly antiquated, the Declaration of Geneva (1948) updated it, while at the same time taking care to include the promise: 'I will maintain the utmost respect for human life from the time of conception'.

One would not necessarily expect a country like Japan, whose Christian population numbers less than 1%, to reflect a biblical view of the sanctity of human life (although of course the Buddhist tradition professes all life to be sacred). So we are not altogether surprised by the statistics which followed their liberalization of abortion legislation in 1948. In the first eight years no fewer than five million abortions were performed, and in the year 1972 the number had increased to one and a half millions.[4]

But in the West, the heir of many centuries of Christian tradition, one's expectations are naturally higher. In England abortion remained illegal until the Infant Life (Preservation) Act of 1929 provided that no action would be punishable 'when done in good faith with the intention of saving the life of the mother'. Mr David Steel's 1967 Abortion Act appeared to many to be only a cautious extension of this. Two registered medical practitioners were required to express their opinion, 'formed in good faith', that the continuance of the pregnancy would involve either (1) risk to the life of the pregnant woman, or (2 and 3) risk of injury to her or her existing children's physical or mental health, 'greater than if the pregnancy were terminated', or (4) 'substantial risk that if the child were born it would suffer from such physical or mental abnormalities as to be seriously handicapped'. Whatever the intentions were of the Abortion Law Reform Association (who master-minded the Bill), it seems clear that its catastrophic consequences were not foreseen by its parliamentary sponsors. Before the Act became law, the number of legal abortions carried out annually in the hospitals of the National Health Service in England and Wales crept up slowly to 6,100 (1966).[5] In 1968, however, the number was already 24,000, and the peak of 167,000 was reached in 1973.[6] By 1983 over two million legal abortions had been performed since the 1967 Act was passed.

The situation in the United States is even worse. In 1970 a Texan lady (who used the pseudonym Jane Roe) became pregnant and decided to fight the anti-abortion legislation of her state. She took Henry Wade, the Dallas district attorney, to court. In January 1973 in the now notorious *Roe v. Wade* case, the United States Supreme Court declared by 7 votes to 2 that the Texas law was unconstitutional.[7] Its judgment inhibited all regulation of abortion during the first three months of pregnancy, and during the second and third trimesters regulated it only in relation to the mother's physical or mental health. This ruling implicitly permitted abortion on demand at every stage of pregnancy. The number of legal abortions in the United States in 1969 was less than 20,000. In 1975 it passed the million mark, and in 1980 had reached more than one and a half million. This means that in 1980 for every 1000 'births' (natural and induced), 300 were abortions. In fact, over 4,250 babies are aborted daily, 177 hourly, or three every minute. In Washington DC, the nation's capital, abortions now outnumber live births by three to one.[8]

The total number of legal and illegal abortions throughout the world was estimated in 1968 at between thirty and thirty-five millions.[9] It must have increased further by now.

These figures are so staggering as to defy the imagination. I do not think Francis Schaeffer and Everett Koop are exaggerating when they write of 'The Slaughter of the Innocents', or John Powell SJ when he entitles his moving book *Abortion: The Silent Holocaust*.[10] To make his point yet more forcefully, he introduces his book with a chart of 'war casualties', on which each cross represents 50,000 American combatants killed. The Korean and Vietnam wars have only one cross each. World War I has two and a half, and World War II eleven. But 'the War on the Unborn' has no fewer than 240 crosses, representing the 12 million legal American abortions up to the beginning of 1981.

Any society which can tolerate these things, let alone legislate for them, has ceased to be civilized. One of the major signs of decadence in the Roman Empire was that its unwanted babies were 'exposed', that is, abandoned and left to die. Can we claim that contemporary western society is any less decadent because it consigns its unwanted babies to the hospital incinerator instead of the local rubbish dump? Indeed modern abortion is even worse than ancient exposure in this respect that it has been commercialized, and has become, at least for some doctors and clinics, an extremely lucrative practice.[11] But reverence for human life is an indispensable characteristic of a humane and civilized society.

The Key Issue

Those who campaign for a lax policy on abortion, and those who campaign for a strict one, begin their argument from opposite positions.

Pro-abortionists emphasize the rights of the mother, and especially her right to choose; anti-abortionists emphasize the rights of the unborn child, and especially his or her right to live. The first see abortion as little more than a retroactive contraceptive, the second as little less than pre-natal infanticide. The appeal of pro-abortionists is usually to compassion (though also to the justice of what they see as a woman's rights); they cite situations in which the mother and/or the rest of the existing family would suffer intolerable strain if an unwanted pregnancy were allowed to come to term. The appeal of anti-abortionists is usually also and especially to justice; they stress the need to defend the rights of the unborn child who is unable to defend himself.

Those who oppose easy abortion are not lacking in compassion, however. They recognize the hardships, and even tragedies, which the arrival of an unplanned baby often brings. For example, an expectant mother is already worn out by a large and demanding family. Their home is already over-crowded and their budget over-stretched. It would be financially crippling to have another mouth to feed. The family simply could not cope with another child. Or the mother is herself the wage earner (because she is widowed or divorced, or her husband is sick or unemployed); to have another child would ruin the family. Or the husband is violent or cruel, perhaps an alcoholic or even a psychopath, and his wife dare not allow another child to come under his influence. Or she is unmarried and feels she cannot face either the stigma or the disadvantage which she and her child would have to endure in a single-parent family. Or she is a schoolgirl or student, and a continued pregnancy would interfere with her education and her career. Or perhaps her pregnancy is due to adultery or incest or rape, and these tragedies are great enough in themselves without adding to them an unplanned, unwanted child. Or she has contracted rubella, or had a prenatal scan, and fears that her child will be a mongol or defective in some other way.

All these cases, and many more, cause great personal suffering, and arouse our sincere Christian compassion. It is easy to understand why some women in such situations opt for the abortion which seems to them the only escape, and why some doctors interpret the law as liberally as they can, in order to justify one.

But Christians who confess Jesus as Lord, and who desire to live under the authority of his truth, justice and compassion, can never be pure pragmatists. We have to ask ourselves what principles are involved. Our compassion needs both theological and moral guidelines. If it is expressed at the expense of truth or justice, it ceases to be genuine compassion.

The key issue, then, is a moral and theological one. It concerns the nature of the foetus (*foetus* is Latin for 'offspring'). How are we to think of the embryo in the mother's womb? For it is our evaluation of the foetus which will largely determine our attitude to abortion. Furthermore, although other questions of principle are involved in genetic engineering, *in vitro* fertilization and embryo experimentation, and I am not intending to address these issues in this chapter, yet in these areas too the main question is the same: what is the status before God of a fertilized ovum, whether in the womb or in a test tube?

We reject as totally false and utterly abhorrent the notion that the foetus is merely a lump of jelly or blob of tissue, or a growth in the mother's womb, which may therefore be extracted and destroyed like teeth, tumours or tonsils. Yet some appear to adopt this extreme position. For example, K. Hindell and Madelaine Simms (pro-abortion campaigners) have written that 'medically and legally the embryo and foetus are merely parts of the mother's body, and not yet human'.[12] Such people insist that the foetus belongs to the woman who bears it; that it cannot be regarded as in any sense independent of her or as human in its own right; that to have it removed is no more significant than the surgical removal of some other unwanted tissue; and that the decision to abort or not to abort rests entirely with the woman. Since it is her body, it is also her choice. Nobody else (and certainly no man, feminists would add) has any say in the matter. A liberated woman cannot be forced to bear a child; she has absolute control over her own reproductive powers and processes.

After a mass rally in Hyde Park, arranged by the Society for the Protection of Unborn Children in June 1983, we were walking to 10 Downing Street, in order to present a petition to the Prime Minister, when at the top of Whitehall a group of young women started chanting –

Not the Church, not the State,
Let the woman decide her fate.

I went over to talk to them, and quietly remonstrated that it was not the woman's fate we were concerned about in our rally and march, so much as her unborn child's. Their only reply was to shout unprintable obscenities at me, and to make the rather obvious point that I would not be able to give birth to a child in a million years. I am not saying that they were wholly wrong. For I recognize that abortion is more a woman's issue than a man's. It is she who has been made pregnant, perhaps without her consent, who has to bear the pregnancy, and who will carry the burden of early child care. It is all too easy for a man to forget these facts. Nevertheless, her child has independent rights both before and after birth, and it is these rights which those young women in Whitehall did not acknowledge.

That an embryo, though carried within the mother's body, is nevertheless not a part of it, is not only a theological but a physiological fact. This is partly because the child has a genotype distinct from the mother's, but also because the whole process of gestation, from ovulation to birth, may be seen as a kind of 'expulsion' of the child with a view to its ultimate independence.

There is a second group of people who seek the decisive moment of the embryo's 'humanization' at some point between conception and birth. Some opt for implantation when the egg, four or five days after fertilization, descends the fallopian tube and becomes attached to the wall of the uterus. And it is true both that implantation is an indispensable stage in the development of the foetus, and that the greatest number of spontaneous abortions (often due to foetal abnormality) takes place before this moment. Nevertheless, implantation changes only the environment of the foetus, not its constitution. In former generations 'quickening' was regarded by many as the moment of, or at least the evidence for, the 'ensoulment' of the embryo, but we now know that this new beginning is not of the child's movement but of the mother's perception of it. A third option is 'viability', the time when the foetus, if born prematurely, would be able to survive. But modern medical techniques are constantly bringing this moment forward. The fourth option is to regard birth itself as the crucial moment. This was the position adopted by Rex Gardner in his *Abortion: The Personal*

Dilemma (1972). 'My own view,' he wrote, 'is that while the foetus is to be cherished increasingly as it develops, we should regard its first breath at birth as the moment when God gives it not only life, but the offer of Life.' He quoted Genesis 2.7 as biblical evidence, when God breathed into man's nostrils 'the breath of life'. He appealed also to common human experience: 'an audible sigh of relief goes round the delivery room when the baby gives that first gasp'.[13] It is certainly true that no funeral is held for a stillborn child, and that Scripture usually speaks of 'new life' beginning at 'new birth'. Yet this does not settle the matter, since Scripture also speaks of God 'begetting' us and of the implanted 'seed' which leads to new birth.[14] In addition, pictures of the child just before birth reveal that there is no fundamental difference between the unborn and the newly born: both are dependent on their mother, although in a different way.

The third group of people, which I think should include all Christians, although they use different formulations and draw different deductions, looks back to conception or fusion as the decisive moment when a human being begins. This is the official position of the Roman Catholic Church. Pope Pius XII, for example, in his Address to the Italian Catholic Society of Midwives in 1951, said: 'The baby, still not born, is a man in the same degree and for the same reason as the mother.'[15] Similarly, many Protestants, although some find difficulty with the non-recognition of 'degree', yet similarly affirm that there is no point between conception and death at which we can say 'after that point I was a person, but before it I was not'. For certainly the conceptus is alive, and certainly the life it possesses is human life. Indeed, many medical people who make no Christian profession recognize this fact. Thus the First International Conference on Abortion, meeting in 1967 in Washington DC, declared: 'We can find no point in time between the union of sperm and egg and the birth of an infant at which point we can say that this is not a human life.'[16]

The Biblical Basis

To me the firmest foundation in Scripture for this view is to be found in Psalm 139, in which the author marvels at God's omniscience and omnipresence, and in the course of his meditation makes important statements about our prenatal existence. To be sure, Psalm 139 makes no claim to be a textbook of embryology. It employs poetical imagery and highly figurative language, (e.g. verse 15 'I was woven together in the depths of the earth'). Nevertheless, the psalmist is affirming at least three important truths.

The first concerns his *Creation*. 'You created my inmost being; you knit me together in my mother's womb' (verse 13). Two homely metaphors are used to illustrate God's creative skill, namely the potter and the weaver. God is like a skilled artisan, who 'created' (or better 'formed') him as the potter works the clay. The same thought recurs in Job 10.8, where Job affirms that God's hands had 'fashioned and made' him (RSV) or 'shaped and modelled' him (JB). The other picture is that of the weaver who 'knit' him together (verse 13), which the NASB renders 'thou didst weave me'. Similarly Job asks: 'Did you not . . . clothe me with skin and flesh, and knit me together with bones and sinews?' (10.10, 11). In consequence, the psalmist goes on: 'For all these mysteries I thank you, for the wonder of myself, for the wonder of your works' (verse 14, JB).

Though not intending to give a scientific account of foetal development, the biblical authors are nevertheless affirming (in the familiar imagery of the Ancient Near East) that the process of embryonic growth is neither haphazard nor even automatic, but a divine work of creative skill.

The psalmist's second emphasis is on *Continuity*. He is now an adult, but he looks back over his life until before he was born. He refers to himself both before and after birth by the same personal pronouns 'I' and 'me', for he is aware that during his antenatal and postnatal life he was and is the same person. He surveys his existence in four stages. First (verse

1), 'you have searched me' (the past). Secondly (verses 2, 3), 'you know when I sit and when I rise, . . . you are familiar with all my ways' (the present). Thirdly (verse 10), 'your hand will guide me, your right hand will hold me fast' (the future). And fourthly (verse 13), 'you knit me together in my mother's womb' (the pre-natal stage). Yet in all four stages (before birth, from birth to the present, at the present moment, and in the future), he refers to himself as 'I'. He who is thinking and writing as a grown man has the same personal identity as the foetus in the womb. He is aware of no discontinuity between his antenatal and postnatal being. On the contrary, in and out of his mother's womb, before and after his birth, as embryo, baby, youth and adult, he is conscious of being the same person.

The third truth the psalmist expresses I will term *Communion*, for he is conscious of a very personal and particular communion between God and himself. It is the same God who created him, who now sustains him, knows him and loves him, and who will forever hold him fast. Psalm 139 is perhaps the most radically personal statement in the Old Testament of God's relationship to the individual believer. The 'I-you' relationship is expressed in almost every line. Either the pronoun or the possessive in the first person ('I – me – my') comes forty-six times in the psalm, and in the second person ('you – your') thirty-two times. More important than the 'I – you' relationship is his awareness of the 'you – me' relationship, of God knowing him, surrounding him, holding him (verses 1–6), and of God sticking to him in covenant faithfulness and never leaving him or letting him go (verses 7–12).

Indeed, 'Communion' may not be the best description of this third awareness, because the word implies a reciprocal relationship, whereas the psalmist is bearing witness to a relationship which God has established and which God sustains. Perhaps therefore 'Covenant' would be a better word, indeed a unilateral covenant, or covenant of 'grace' which God initiated and which God maintains. For God our

Creator loved us and related himself to us long before we could respond in a conscious relationship to him. What makes us a person, then, is not that we know God, but that he knows us; not that we love God but that he has set his love upon us. So each of us was already a person in our mother's womb, because already then God knew us and loved us.

It is these three words (Creation, Continuity and Communion or Covenant) which give us the essential biblical perspective from which to think. The foetus is neither a growth in the mother's body, nor even a potential human being, but already a human life who, though not yet mature, has the potentiality of growing into the fullness of the individual humanity he *already* possesses.

Other biblical passages express the same sense of personal continuity due to divine grace. Several times in the Wisdom Literature of the Old Testament the conviction is expressed that it is God who 'made me in the womb' (Job. 31.15; Ps. 119.73), even though we do not know how (Eccle. 11.5), who 'brought me out of the womb', and who therefore 'from my mother's womb' has been my God (Psalm 22.9, 10; 71.6). The prophets shared the same belief, whether of the individual like Jeremiah ('before I formed you in the womb I knew you', 1.5), or of 'the Servant of the Lord' (whom the Lord both formed and called in the womb, Isa. 49.1, 5) or by analogy of the nation of Israel (Isa. 46.3, 4). The implications of these texts for personal continuity cannot be avoided by analogy with New Testament assertions that God 'chose' us in Christ and 'gave' us his grace in Christ 'before the creation of the world' (e.g. Eph. 1.4; 2 Tim. 1.9). The argument would then be that, just as we did not exist before the beginning of time except in the mind of God, so we had no personal existence in the womb, although God is said to have 'known' us in both cases. The analogy is inexact, however, for the situations are different. In passages which relate to *election*, the emphasis is on salvation by grace not works, and therefore on God's choice of us before we existed or could do any good works. In passages which relate to *vocation*, however (whether the calling of prophets like Jeremiah or of apostles like Paul – cf. Gal. 1.16), the emphasis is not only on God's gracious choice but on his 'forming' or 'fashioning' them for their particular service. This was not 'before the creation of the world', nor even 'before conception', but rather 'before birth', before they were yet fully 'formed', that is, while they were still being 'fashioned' in the womb. Personal continuity before and after birth is integral to this teaching.

There is only one Old Testament passage which some interpreters have thought to devalue the human foetus, namely Exodus 21.22–25.[17] The situation envisaged is not in dispute. While two men are fighting, they accidentally hit a pregnant woman with the result that she either miscarries or 'gives birth prematurely' (NIV). The penalty laid down depends on the seriousness of any injury sustained. If the injury is not serious, a fine is to be imposed; if it is serious, there is to be exact retribution, 'life for life' etc. Some have argued that the first category (no serious injury) means the death of the child, while the second is serious harm to the mother, and that therefore the mere imposition of a fine in the former case indicates that the foetus was regarded as less valuable than the mother. This is a gratuitous interpretation, however. It seems much more probable that the scale of penalty was to correspond to the degree of injury, whether to the mother or to her child, in which case mother and child are valued equally.

Turning to the New Testament, it has often been pointed out not just that when Mary and Elizabeth met, both being pregnant, Elizabeth's baby (John the Baptist) 'leaped in her womb' in salutation of Mary's baby, Jesus, but that Luke here uses the same word *brephos* of an unborn child (1.41, 44) as he later uses of the newborn baby (2.12, 16) and of the little ones whom people brought to Jesus to bless (18.15).

It is fully in keeping with all this implied continuity, that Christian tradition affirms of Jesus Christ in the Apostles' Creed that he was 'conceived by the Holy Spirit, born of the Virgin Mary, suffered under Pontius Pilate, was crucified, dead and buried, . . . and on the third day he rose again. . .'. Throughout these events, from beginning to end, Jesus was and is the very same Jesus who was conceived in the womb of his virgin mother.

Modern medical science appears to confirm this biblical teaching. It was only in the 1960s that the genetic code was unravelled. Now we know that the moment the ovum is fertilized by the penetration of the sperm, the twenty-three pairs of chromosomes are complete, the zygote has a unique genotype which is distinct from both parents, and the child's sex, size and shape, colour of skin, hair and eyes, temperament and intelligence are already determined. Each human being begins as a single fertilized cell, while an adult has about thirty million million cells. Between these two points (fusion and maturity) forty-five generations of cell division are necessary, and forty-one of them occur *before birth*.

Prenatal medical photography has further disclosed the marvels of foetal development. I have in mind particularly the strikingly beautiful pictures in the Swedish photographer Lennart Nilsson's book *A Child is Born*.[18] At three to three and a half weeks the tiny heart begins to beat. At four, though the foetus is only about a quarter of an inch long, the head and body are distinguishable, as are also the rudimentary eyes, ears and mouth. At six or seven weeks brain function can be detected, and at eight (the time abortions begin to be performed) all the child's limbs are apparent, including fingers, fingerprints and toes. At nine or ten weeks the baby can use its hands to grasp and its mouth to swallow, and can even suck its thumb. By thirteen weeks, the completion of the first trimester, the embryo is completely organized, and a miniature baby lies in the mother's womb; he can alter his position, respond to pain, noise and light, and even get a fit of hiccups. From then on the child merely develops in size and strength. By the end of the fifth month and beginning of the sixth (before the second trimester is complete, and while the pregnancy is not yet two-thirds complete), the baby has hair, eyelashes, nails and nipples, and can cry, grip, punch and kick (which sometimes happens after an abortion has been performed by hysterotomy, to the extreme distress of the medical team).

Expectant mothers endorse from their own experience their sense of bearing a living child. True, parents sometimes give their little one a humorous nickname, especially if they do not know which sex it will turn out to be. But they also say with pride, 'We have a baby on the way.' During pregnancy one mother said she 'felt herself to be the mother of a person, with certain motherly responsibilities before birth, and others after birth'. Another wrote: 'My feelings know that this is a person, and thus has his or her own independent rights before God.'

A Contemporary Christian Debate

It would not be honest to claim that all Christians see eye to eye on this issue, even all Christians who seek to submit to the authority of Scripture. An apparently sharp difference of opinion has surfaced since an interdisciplinary seminar of theologians and doctors was held in 1983, jointly sponsored by the London Institute for Contemporary Christianity and the Christian Medical Fellowship. The keynote address was given by Canon Oliver O'Donovan, Regius Professor of Moral and Pastoral Theology at Oxford, under the title 'And who is a Person?' His starting point was the Parable of the Good Samaritan. Just as Jesus declined to answer the question 'and who is my neighbour?' by providing a set of criteria, so there are no criteria (whether self-consciousness or reason or responsive love) by which to decide who is a 'person'. Instead, the Good Samaritan identified his neighbour by caring for him, since 'the truth of neighbourhood is known in engagement'. Just so, the question, 'Who is a person?' cannot be answered speculatively. Instead, we come to *recognise* someone as a person 'only from a stance of prior moral commitment to treat him or her as a person'. Then later we come to *know* him or her as a person, as he or she is disclosed to us in personal relationships. It is not that personhood is *conferred* on someone by our resolve to treat him as a person, but that personhood is *disclosed* that way. Personhood becomes apparent in personal relationships, although it is not established by them. At the same time, before we commit ourselves to the service of a person, it is right to look for evidence that it is appropriate to do so, either by appearance or (in the case of a foetus) by our scientific knowledge of its unique genotype. There are thus three stages. First, there must be recognition, making it appropriate to engage with a person as person. Next follows commitment, caring for him as a person. And thirdly there comes encounter: 'Those whom we *treat* as persons when they are yet unborn, become *known* to us as persons when they are children'. These three stages acknowledge the gradualness of development into personal encounter, while affirming the reality of personhood from the moment of conception.[19]

In an unpublished essay entitled 'The Logic of Beginnings' Professor Donald MacKay, director of the Research Department of Communication and Neuroscience at Keele University, takes issue with Professor O'Donovan's argument. 'Things come into existence in various ways,' he writes. For example, artefacts (like a car) are assembled piece by piece, rain clouds form by condensation, an explosive mixture of gas and air develops gradually, while plants and animals grow. Each of these processes has an end product (a car, a raincloud, an explosion, a mature plant or an animal), but it is difficult for us to perceive either the exact moment when this comes into being or the exact nature of the change which takes place when it does. This leads Donald MacKay to criticize the language of 'potentiality'. To be sure, the beginning of every process has the potentiality to reach the end product, granted the enabling conditions, but this does not justify ontological assertions about the earlier stages. For example, various components will become a car, if they are assembled properly, but we do not refer to them as a 'potential car', because they might instead end up on the scrapheap. May we then refer to a fertilized ovum as a 'potential human being'? Yes, in the sense that it will lead to maturity if gestation proceeds normally, but no if this leads us to attribute to the ovum the specific properties of the end product. The value of 'potentiality' language is that it emphasizes the importance of beginnings, expectations and resulting obligations; its danger is to imagine that all the attributes and rights of the end product already belong to the beginning. They do not, even if there is a direct line of continuity between the two.

In particular, Donald MacKay concludes, before the foetus may rightly be considered a 'conscious personal agency', there are certain information-processing requirements which are necessary for human self-supervision. This is not to reduce a person to a brain, but to say that a person cannot be embodied in a structure which lacks a self-supervisory system because it lacks adequate brain development. 'The capacity to sustain conscious personhood is a systemic property of the central nervous system.' On the one hand, the fertilized ovum is a 'physical structure with the richest and most strangely mysterious repertoire known to man', for it can develop into 'the embodiment of a new human being in the image of God, loved by God, replete with potentialities of not merely earthly but eternal significance'. On the other, to treat it as 'a person with the rights of a person' is a conspicuous example of 'thin-end-of-the-wedgery'.[20]

In summary, Oliver O'Donovan insists that the foetus has 'personhood' from the moment of fusion, and that therefore we must commit ourselves to its care, although only later will its personhood be revealed in personal relationships. Donald MacKay agrees that from the moment of fusion the conceptus has biological life and a marvellous repertoire of potentiality, but only becomes a person possessing rights and demanding care when brain development makes self-supervision possible.

The conflict between the two learned Professors sounds irreconcileable. Yet I believe that there may be more common ground between them than appears at first sight, and I do not believe that either is altogether denying what the other affirms. Donald MacKay emphasizes the development of the foetus, while not denying that already the fertilized ovum has a rich repertoire. Oliver O'Donovan emphasizes that from the very beginning the conceptus has a unique and complete genotype, and indeed personhood, while not denying that its destiny is to reach human maturity. Is this not at base the old tension (with which the New Testament has made us familiar) between the 'already' and the 'not yet'? Tertullian expressed it as early as the end of the second century: 'He also is a man who is about to be one; you have the fruit already in its seed'.[21] In our own day Paul Ramsey has put it like this: 'The human individual comes into existence as a minute informational speck. . . . His subsequent prenatal and postnatal development may be described as *a process of becoming what he already is* from the moment he was conceived'.[22] Lewis Smedes calls the status of a foetus a 'deep ontological ambiguity – the ambiguity of not being something yet and at the same time having the makings of what it will be'.[23]

This brings me back to Psalm 139 and to the reason for the psalmist's sense of continuity of being, namely God's steadfast love. Indeed, it is God's loving, personal commitment to the unborn child which makes me uncomfortable with Donald MacKay's non-personal analogies (material artefacts, clouds, gases, plants and animals). The sovereign initiative of God in creating and loving is the biblical understanding of grace. Donald MacKay declines to attribute personhood to the newly conceived foetus because as yet it has no brain to sustain either self-supervision or conscious relationships. But supposing the vital relationship which confers personhood on the foetus is God's conscious, loving commitment to him, rather than his to God? Such a one-sided relationship is seen in parents who love their child, and commit themselves to its care and protection, long before it is able to respond. And a unilateral initiative is what makes grace to be grace. It is, in fact, God's grace which confers on the unborn child, from the moment of its conception, both the unique status which it already enjoys and the unique destiny which it will later inherit. It is grace which holds together this duality of the actual and the potential, the already and the not yet.

Implications and Conclusions

How will our evaluation of the uniqueness of the human foetus (however we decide to formulate it) affect our thinking and acting?

To begin with, it will change our attitudes. Since the life of the human foetus is a human life, with the potential of becoming a mature human being, we have to learn to think of mother and unborn child as two human beings at different stages of development. Doctors and nurses have to consider that they have two patients, not one, and must seek the well-being of both. Lawyers and politicians need to think similarly. As the United Nations' 'Declaration of the Rights of the Child' (1959) put it, the child needs 'special safeguards and care, including appropriate legal protection, before as well as after birth'. Christians would wish to add 'extra care before birth'. For the Bible has much to say about God's concern for the defenceless, and the most defenceless of all people are unborn children. They are speechless to plead their own cause and helpless to protect their own life. So it is our responsibility to do for them what they cannot do for themselves.

All Christians should therefore be able to agree that the human foetus is in principle inviolable. Lord Ramsey, when as Archbishop of Canterbury he was addressing the Church Assembly in 1967, said: 'We have to assert as normative the general inviolability of the foetus. . . . We shall be right to continue to see as one of Christianity's great gifts to the world the belief that the human foetus is to be reverenced as the embryo of a life capable of coming to reflect the glory of God. . . .'

It is this combination of what the human foetus already is and one day could be which makes the realities of abortion so horrific. How can anybody conceivably reconcile the brutal techniques of abortion with the concept of the abortus as a potential mirror of God's glory? The oldest method is 'D and C', dilation and curettage. The cervix is dilated to facilitate the insertion of an implement, either a 'curette' with which the wall of the womb is scraped until the foetus is cut into pieces, or a suction tube by which it is torn into pieces. In either case a violent and bloody dismemberment takes place. The second method (employed between twelve and sixteen weeks after conception) is to inject a toxic (usually saline) solution by a long needle inserted through the mother's abdomen into the amniotic sac enveloping the foetus, which is thus poisoned, burned and killed, and then 'spontaneously' ejected. At a later stage of pregnancy surgery is used, either a hysterotomy which resembles a Caesarean section (except that in this case the baby is taken from the womb to be killed, not saved) or a complete hysterectomy by which womb and foetus are removed together and discarded together. A fourth method, an alternative to surgery, is the use of prostaglandin, a hormone which induces immediate premature delivery, often of a live baby.

A factual knowledge of these procedures should lead us to revise our vocabulary. For the popular euphemisms make it easier for us to conceal the truth from ourselves. The occupant of the mother's womb is not a 'product of conception' or 'gametic material', but an unborn child. Even 'pregnancy' tells us no more than that a woman has been 'impregnated', whereas the truth in old-fashioned language is that she is 'with child'. How can we speak of 'the termination of a pregnancy' when what is terminated is not just the mother's pregnancy but the child's life? And how can we describe the average abortion today as 'therapeutic' (a word originally used only when the mother's life was at stake), when pregnancy is not a disease needing therapy, and what abortion effects nowadays is not a cure but a killing? And how can people think of abortion as no more than a kind of contraceptive, when what it does is not prevent conception but destroy the conceptus?

We need to have the courage to use accurate language. Induced abortion is foeticide, the deliberate destruction of an unborn child, the shedding of innocent blood.

Is abortion, then, never justified? To answer this question in a way that is both faithful and realistic, theologians and doctors need each other. More interdisciplinary consultation is necessary. For doctors are understandably impatient with theologians because they tend to be unpractical, making ivory-tower pronouncements unrelated to painful clinical dilemmas. Theologians, on the other hand, are understandably impatient with doctors because they tend to be pragmatists, making clinical decisions uncontrolled by theological principle. The principle on which we should be able to agree is well expressed as the first aim of the Society for the Protection of Unborn Children, namely 'that human life ought not to be taken except in cases of urgent necessity'. Professor G. R. Dunstan is probably right that there is an ethic of 'justifiable foeticide', by analogy with 'justifiable homicide'.[24] But if we accept the general inviolability of the human foetus, then every exception has to be rigorously and specifically argued. Ever since the Infant Life (Preservation) Act (1929) an abortion to save the mother's life has been legal in England, though not condoned by the Roman Catholic Church. With improved modern medical techniques, however, this case hardly ever arises, although one could imagine a borderline situation in which an unwanted pregnancy threatened an overburdened and neurotic mother with such a complete breakdown, that she would become 'a physical and mental wreck',[25] or seems to be in imminent danger of taking her own life. According to Christian tradition human life may be taken to protect and preserve another life, e.g. in self-defence; we have no liberty to introduce death into a situation in which it does not exist or is not threatened.

What about the 'substantial risk' of the child to be born being 'seriously handicapped', which is the fourth clause of the 1967 Abortion Act? Antenatal screening and amniocentesis (tapping and testing the amniotic fluid) can now reveal abnormalities in the foetus at about the fourth month. Is an abortion then morally justified? Many think so. Dr Glanville Williams has expressed himself forcefully on this issue: 'To allow the breeding of defectives is a horrible evil, far worse than any that may be found in abortion.'[26] In discussing the tragic predicament of a mother who gives birth to 'a viable monster or an idiot child', he even wrote: 'An eugenic killing by a mother, exactly paralleled by the bitch that kills her misshapen puppies, cannot confidently be pronounced immoral.'[27] How should a Christian conscience react to this possibility? Surely with horror. The only exception would be an anencephalic child (born without a brain) or a child so completely malformed as to be incapable of independent survival; these could be allowed to die, for in such cases the foetus is recognized as being non-human and is generally referred to as a 'monster'.

But there are at least three reasons why such a drastic procedure must be reserved for only the most exceptional cases and must not be extended to other – even severe – abnormalities. First, it is now frequently said that the issue is not the 'sanctity' of life but the 'quality' of life, and that the life of a severely handicapped person is not worth living. But who can presume to decide this? To me the most moving speech at the Hyde Park Rally in June 1983, which I have already mentioned, was made by Alison Davis, who described herself as 'a happy spina bifida adult' and spoke from a wheelchair. 'I can think of few concepts more terrifying,' she said, 'than saying that certain people are better off dead, and may therefore be killed *for their own good*.' One doctor, on hearing her say that she was glad to be alive, 'made the incredible observation that no one can judge their own quality of life, and that other people might well consider a life like mine miserable!' On the contrary, she insisted, 'most handicapped people are quite contented with the quality of their lives'. After all, it is love which gives quality to life and makes it worth living, and it is we – their neighbours – who can choose whether to give love to the handicapped or withhold it. The quality of their life is in our hands.

Secondly, once we accept that a handicapped child may be destroyed before birth, why should we not do it also after birth? Indeed, the practice of infanticide has already begun. Doctors of course do not use this word, and some try to persuade themselves that starving babies to death is not killing them, but 'I'd like to bet they'd change their minds,' said Alison Davis, 'if we did it to them!' The solemn fact is that if society is prepared to kill an unborn child on the sole ground that it will be handicapped, there is no logical reason why we should not go on to kill the deformed newborn, the comatose victim of a car crash, the imbecile and the senile. For the handicapped become disposable when their lives are judged 'worthless' or 'unproductive', and we are back in Hitler's horrible Third Reich.

Christians will rather agree with Jean Rostan, the French biologist, who wrote: 'For my part I believe that there is no life so degraded, debased, deteriorated or impoverished that it does not deserve respect and is not worth defending with zeal and conviction . . . I have the weakness to believe that it is an honour for our society to desire the expensive luxury of sustaining life for its useless, incompetent, and incurably ill members. I would almost measure society's degree of civilization by the amount of effort and vigilance it imposes on itself out of pure respect for life.'[28]

A third reason for not aborting the handicapped is that to do so would be for fallible mortals to play God. We do not have that authority, and those who arrogate it to themselves are bound to make grave mistakes. Maurice Baring used to tell the story of one doctor who asked another: 'About the termination of a pregnancy, I want your opinion. The father was syphilitic, the mother tuberculous. Of the four children born the first was blind, the second died, the third was deaf and dumb, and the fourth also tuberculous. What would you have done?' 'I would have ended the pregnancy'. 'Then you would have murdered Beethoven.'[29]

In this whole discussion we have to be on our guard against selfish rationalizations. I fear that the real reason why we say that serious handicap would be an unbearable burden for a child, if it were allowed to be born, is that it would be an unbearable burden for us. But Christians must remember that the God of the Bible has expressed his special protective care for the handicapped and weak.

What then shall we do? First, *we need to repent*. I agree with Raymond Johnston, the director of CARE Trust,[31] when he wrote in a newspaper article: 'I personally am convinced that the destruction of the unborn on this massive, deliberate scale is the greatest single offence regularly perpetrated in Britain today, and would be the *first* thing an Old Testament prophet *redivivus* would reproach us for.' Dr Francis Schaeffer and Dr Everett Koop dedicated their book and film *Whatever Happened to the Human Race?* 'To those who were robbed of life, the unborn, the weak, the sick, the old, during the dark ages of madness, selfishness, lust and greed for which the last decades of the twentieth century are remembered.' Were they right to condemn our 'enlightened' western civilization as 'the dark ages'? At least in this matter I think they were, and I for one am ashamed that we Christians have not been 'the light of the world' which Jesus intended us to be.

Secondly, *we must accept full responsibility for the effects of a tighter abortion policy*, if it can be secured. To agitate for it without being prepared to bear its cost would be sheer hypocrisy. We must not occasion an increase of illegal 'back street' abortions. Instead, we shall want to help the pregnant woman to overcome any reluctance she feels to have her baby, and see that she is given every possible personal, medical, social and financial support. For God tells us to 'carry each other's burdens, and in this way . . . fulfil the law of Christ' (Gal. 6.2). We shall want to ensure that, although some babies are unwanted (and even unloved) by their parents, no baby is unwanted by society in general and by the church in particular. We should not hesitate to oppose the abortion, and urge the birth, of every child. Pregnancy is a time of emotional instability, so that the minds and feelings of expectant mothers sometimes change. Rex Gardner refers to two reports about women who have been refused an abortion. In one case 73% of them, in the other 84%, said they were glad the pregnancy had not been terminated. He also quotes Sir John Stallworthy that some of the happiest people he knows are those who have said to him: 'You don't remember, but the first time I came wanting an abortion. Thank God you did not agree, because this child has brought the greatest joy into our home that we have ever known.'[30] As for those who would find the strain of keeping their child too great, there is a lengthy queue of married but infertile couples who are longing for the chance to adopt. As Mother Teresa says, 'we are fighting abortion by adoption'.

I thank God for the organizations which have been pioneering a supportive ministry for pregnant women, like 'Birthright' in Canada and the United States, 'Alternatives to Abortion International' (whose publication is called *Heartbeat*), and LIFE and SPUC (Society for the Protection of Unborn Children) in England.[31] In different ways they are offering a caring service, such as counselling women with an unplanned pregnancy, offering emergency help to those in despair, giving advice on practical problems, finding accommodation for mothers both before and after their child's birth, helping to secure employment for them, granting financial help, and providing personal support groups. As Louise Summerhill, founder of 'Birthright' has written, 'We help rather than abort, we believe in making a better world for babies to come into, rather than killing them.'[32]

Thirdly, *we need to support a positive educational and social campaign*. Christians must not be shy to teach thoroughly and constantly the biblical understanding of humanness and of the value, indeed the sacredness, of human life. We have to recognize that all abortions are due to unwanted pregnancies, and that all unwanted pregnancies are due to a failure of some kind.

Often it is sexual failure, whether lack of sexual self-control (especially in men, who usually escape the tragic consequences of their action) or lack of a responsible use of contraceptives. The Church of England General Synod's Board for Social Responsibility has called for 'a major effort at social education' (and moral education too, we might add), in order 'to reduce the number of unwanted pregnancies', 'to undermine the habit of mind which leads straight from the recognition of pregnancy to resort to an abortionist', and to move the public 'to find a better solution'.[33] This is 'The Better Way' of which Rex Gardner writes in his chapters 28 and 29.[34]

Unwelcome pregnancies are also often due to social failure, to such conditions as poverty, unemployment and overcrowding. So for this reason too we should be working for a better society. Social evils are to be fought; they will not be solved by more abortions.

More important in the end than either social education or social action, vital as they both are, is the good news of Jesus Christ. He came to bind up the broken-hearted and support the weak. He calls us to treat all human life with reverence, whether in the unborn, the infant, the handicapped or the senile.

I have no desire to stand in personal judgment either on the women who have resorted to an abortion, or on the men whose sexual self-indulgence is responsible for most unwanted pregnancies. I want to say to them instead, 'There is forgiveness with God' (Ps. 130.4). For Christ died for our sins and offers us a new beginning. He rose again and lives, and by his Spirit can give us a new, inward power of self-control. He is also building a new community characterized by love, joy, peace, freedom and justice. A new beginning. A new power. A new community. This is the gospel of Christ.

Notes

1 Acts 17.25, 28; Ps. 104.29; Job. 1.21.
2 Desmond Doig, *Mother Teresa: Her People and Her Work* (Collins, 1976), p. 162.
3 Francis A. Schaeffer and C. Everett Koop, *Whatever Happened to the*

Human Race? (Revell, 1979; revised British edition by Marshall Morgan & Scott, 1980). See particularly Chapter 1 'The Abortion of the Human Race' (pp. 2–27) and Chapter 4 'The Basis for Human Dignity' (pp. 68–99).

4 The Japanese abortion statistics are given by C. Everett Koop in his *The Right to Live; the Right to Die* (Tyndale House USA and Coverdale House, UK, 1976), p. 46.

5 Report of the Committee on the Working of the Abortion Act 1967, Vol. 1 (HMSO Cmnd. 5579, April 1974), p. 11.

6 The Registrar General's Statistical Review of England and Wales for the years 1968–73; Supplement on 'Abortion' (HMSO).

7 A full description and discussion of the *Roe v. Wade* case may be found in *Death Before Birth* by Harold O. J. Brown (Thomas Nelson, 1977), pp. 73–96.

8 These figures are taken from (1) *Statistical Abstract of the United States: 1982–83* (U.S. Bureau of the Census, 1982) p. 68, and (2) 'Intercessors for America Newsletter', Vol. 10, No. 2 (Feb. 1983).

9 Quoted from Daniel Callahan's *Abortion: Law, Choice and Morality*, p. 298 by Lewis B. Smedes in *Mere Morality* (Eerdmans, 1983), p. 267 footnote 21.

10 John Powell S. J., *Abortion: the Silent Holocaust* (Argus Communications, Allen, Texas, 1981), e.g. pp. 20–39.

11 For ancient perspectives and practices, see *Abortion and the Early Church*, Christian, Jewish and Pagan attitudes in the Graeco-Roman world, by Michael J. Gorman (Inter-Varsity Press, Illinois, 1982).

12 Quoted from *Abortion Law Reformed* (1971) by R. F. R. Gardner in *Abortion: The Personal Dilemma* (Paternoster Press, 1972), p. 62.

13 R. F. R. Gardner, *Abortion: The Personal Dilemma* (Paternoster Press, 1972), p. 126.

14 See, for example, James 1.18; 1 Peter 1.23–25; and 1 John 3.9.

15 Quoted by John T. Noonan in *The Morality of Abortion* (Harvard University Press, 1970), p. 45.

16 Quoted by C. Everett Koop in *The Right to Live; the Right to Die*, pp. 43–44.

17 John M. Frame discusses this passage fully, including the meaning of the Hebrew words used, in his chapter in *Thou Shalt Not Kill*, the Christian Case against Abortion, ed. Richard L. Ganz (Arlington House, 1978), pp. 50–57.

18 First published by Faber in 1965.

19 For Oliver O'Donovan's position see his *The Christian and the Unborn Child* (Grove Booklets on Ethics, No. 1, 1973) and his 1983 London Lectures in Contemporary Christianity *Begotten Not Made?*, Human procreation and medical technique (OUP, 1984).

20 See also Donald MacKay's 1977 London Lectures in Contemporary

Christianity, *Human Science and Human Dignity* (Hodder & Stoughton, 1979), especially pp. 64–5 and 98–102.

21 Tertullian's *Apology*, chapter ix. Michael J. Gorman gives a popular but thorough account of the unanimous pro-life, anti-abortion stance of the first five centuries of Christianity in his *Abortion and the Early Church* (American IVP, 1982). His references to Tertullian are on pp. 54–58.

22 Paul Ramsey, *Fabricated Man*, the ethics of genetic control (Yale University Press, 1970), p. 11.

23 Lewis B. Smedes, *Mere Morality* (Eerdmans, 1983), p. 129.

24 From Professor G. R. Dunstan's contribution to the article on 'Abortion' in the *Dictionary of Medical Ethics*, ed. by A. S. Duncan, G. R. Dunstan and R. B. Welbourn (Darton, Longman and Todd, revised and enlarged edition, 1981).

25 The expression used by Mr Justice McNaughten in the Rex v. Bourne case of 1938.

26 Glanville Williams, *The Sanctity of Life and the Criminal Law* (Faber, 1958), p. 212.

27 ibid. p. 31.

28 Quoted from his book *Humanly Possible* by C. Everett Koop at the beginning of his *The Right to Live; the Right to Die* (q.v).

29 Quoted by Norman St John Stevas in *The Right to Life* (Hodder & Stoughton, 1963), p. 20.

30 op. cit. pp. 225–6.

31 The addresses of these organizations are as follows: 'Birthright', 777 Coxwell Avenue, Toronto, Ontario, Canada, M4C 3C6. Alternatives to Abortion, International, 2606½ West 8th Street, Los Angeles, California 90057, U.S.A. LIFE, 7 The Parade, Leamington Spa, Warwickshire. SPUC, 7 Tufton St., London, SW1. CARE Trust, 21a Down Street, London W1Y 7DN.

32 Quoted by Rex F. R. Gardner in *Abortion: the Personal Dilemma* p. 276. See also *The Story of Birthright: the Alternative to Abortion* by Louise Summerhill (Prow Books, Kenosha, 1973).

33 *Abortion: an Ethical Dilemma*, a report of the Board for Social Responsibility (CIO, 1965), p. 57.

34 op. cit. pp. 248–262.